KT-156-390

AWN

Performance
Management
in a week

PHIL BAGULEY

Hodder Arnold

BROMLEY COLLEGE LIBRARY

B51180

A MEMBER OF THE HODDER HEADLINE GROUP

BROMLEY COLLEGE OF FURTHER & HIGHER EDUCATION	
ACCN.	B51180
CLASSN.	658·3/25
CAT.	LOCN.

Order queries: please contact Bookpoint Ltd, 39 Milton Park, Abingdon, Oxon
Orders: please contact Bookpoint Ltd, 130 Milton Park, Abingdon, Oxon OX14
4SB. Telephone: (44) 01235 827720. Fax: (44) 01235 400454. Lines are open from
9.00–18.00, Monday to Saturday, with a 24 hour message answering service.
You can also order through our website www.hoddereducation.com

British Library Cataloguing in Publication Data
A catalogue record for this title is available from The British Library

ISBN 0 340 849681

First published	2001
Impression number	10 9 8 7 6 5 4 3
Year	2007 2006 2005

Copyright © 2001 Phil Baguley

All rights reserved. Apart from any use permitted under UK copyright law,
this publication may only be reproduced, stored or transmitted, in any form
or by any means, with prior permission in writing of the publisher or in the
case of reprographic production in accordance with the terms of licences
issued by the Copyright Licensing Agency Limited. Further details of such
licences (for reprographic reproduction) may be obtained from the Copyright
Licensing Agency Limited, of 90 Tottenham Court Road, London W1P 4LP.

Typeset by SX Composing DTP, Rayleigh, Essex.
Printed in Great Britain for Hodder Education, a division of Hodder Headline
Plc, 338 Euston Road, London NW1 3BH, by Cox & Wyman Ltd., Reading.

Hodder Headline's policy is to use papers that are natural, renewable and
recyclable products and made from wood grown in sustainable forests. The
logging and manufacturing processes are expected to conform to the
environmental regulations of the country of origin.

chartered

management

institute

inspiring leaders

The leading organisation for professional management

As the champion of management, the Chartered Management Institute shapes and supports the managers of tomorrow. By sharing intelligent insights and setting standards in management development, the Institute helps to deliver results in a dynamic world.

Setting and raising standards

The Institute is a nationally accredited organisation, responsible for setting standards in management and recognising excellence through the award of professional qualifications.

Encouraging development, improving performance

The Institute has a vast range of development programmes, qualifications, information resources and career guidance to help managers and their organisations meet new challenges in a fast-changing environment.

Shaping opinion

With in-depth research and regular policy surveys of its 91,000 individual members and 520 corporate members, the Chartered Management Institute has a deep understanding of the key issues. Its view is informed, intelligent and respected.

For more information call 01536 204222 or visit www.managers.org.uk

■■■■ C O N T E N T S ■■■■

Achieving success in your performance management has much in common with winning the Lottery. They're both worth doing, both much sought after and they both attract a lot of comment and speculation. But, unlike a lottery win, success in your performance management isn't an unlikely, remote event, subject to the fickle whims of chance. For you, successful performance management is a goal that's attainable and achievable. Once you get there, you'll find that it's also maintainable and sustainable. Achieving that goal won't just improve your bottom line, it'll also delight your customers, motivate the people you work with and help your career.

The aim of this book is to provide an easy step-by-step guide to help you to improve the performance of the team, department, section or business that you manage. When you do that, you'll also improve your own performance. The steps that you'll take toward the goal of successful performance management are spread over the seven days of the following week:

Sunday	What is successful performance management?
Monday	People and successful performance management
Tuesday	Quality and successful performance management
Wednesday	Measurement and monitoring for successful performance management
Thursday	Goals, targets and benchmarks for successful performance management
Friday	Successful performance management techniques
Saturday	The long view and review

What is successful performance management?

What goes into it? What are its outcomes and, most important of all, what do you need to have or do in order to achieve success in your performance management?

Finding the right answers to these questions is important. When you find them, they'll enable you to start your journey, the one that will take you to your individual version of successful performance management.

You'll begin that journey today when you look at:

- Why performance management?
- What's performance management about?
- Historic do's and don'ts
- The good news
- People
- Quality   } and
- Measuring and monitoring   Performance
- Goals, targets and benchmarks   Management
- Techniques and tools
- When do you start?
- The ten commandments of successful performance management

Why performance management?

Once upon a time, a long time ago, two of our ancestors – Ug and Mug – were on a hunting trip. Far from their home cave, they came face to face with a large and hungry sabre-toothed tiger. Quick thinking was needed.

'Let's run' said Ug.

'Why bother' said Mug 'it can run faster than us.'

'I know . . .' shouted Ug, already on his way, '. . . but I only need to run faster than you.'

As Ug's descendants, we've carried on the family tradition. The twenty-first century version of this is called performance management. During the week ahead you'll be looking at the hows, whats and whens of performance management. But to start this week you need to recognise a simple, but stark, fact:

Successful performance management is no longer an optional extra.

What's performance management about?

At its core, performance management has three objectives. These are change, change and change! But this change is different; it isn't like the sort of change that you've met before, the sort that's driven by the winds of chance. It's a change that's chosen, a change with a specific objective in mind. It's a change that:

- *is* small, incremental and subtle – rather than huge
- *is* continuous, on-and-on – rather than one-off
- *is* low cost – rather than capital hungry
- *is* understandable, basic and jargon-free – rather than jargonised
- *builds* on people's experience and knowledge
- *is* about bottom-up, people involvement – rather than top-down control

But these are not the only things that make up performance management.

Performance management is driven by the gap between where you are now and where you want to be.

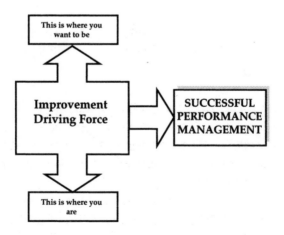

Historic do's and dont's

Let's start your journey to successful performance management by taking a look at some examples of what isn't and, more importantly, what *is* successful performance management. History is littered with examples of poor performance management. If you step back from the debris of these you'll find that most of them *didn't* succeed because they:

- focused on actions rather than results
- had goals that were long-term, wide-span and fuzzy
- rigidly applied a single doctrinaire approach
- involved the use of jargon and mystique
- were top-down controlled and involved 'big buck' spends.

Finding examples of successful performance management is much more difficult. But when you do find them, you'll see that they:

- had low, or even no, capital spend
- had goals that were measurable and achievable
  - *to reduce the reject level to 10% by end June, or*
  - *to increase hotel bedroom occupancy levels by 5% by month end*
- used success to create more success
  - *our Scunthorpe branch used this method to reduce stock losses by half – why don't you?*

- looked for results *now*
  - *what have you done today to improve this shop's sales performance?*
- empowered people
  - *people are quality*
  - *take every opportunity to grab the imagination of your employees*

These – the success stories of performance management – tell you that successful performance management is something that's accessible. You don't need to be a rocket scientist or a genius to be successful at your performance management.

The good news

But what do these stories tell you about the process of performance management and, more importantly, what do they tell you about your chances of getting it right? The answers are good news, news that tells you successful performance management is:

- an act of empowerment for everyone involved
- an opportunity for you to grow, develop and change
- an opportunity for your organization to change and grow.

But that isn't all. For the skills and abilities that you need to achieve success in your performance management are those you've already got. They are the skills and abilities that you use to:

- manage your people and the quality of their work
- measure and monitor that work
- set and strive for the goals, targets and benchmarks of that work
- select and use techniques and tools to help you.

The process of performance management integrates these, linking them together.

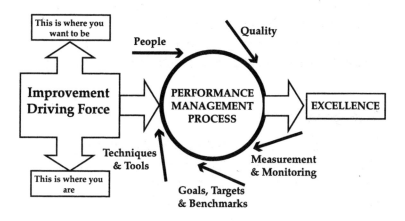

People

People are the core of the process of successful performance management. They go through it – all the way – like the letters in a stick of rock. But their involvement isn't an automatic, built-in-the-genes, job. If you're going to be successful in your performance management, you're going to have to learn how to:

- do it *with* these people rather than *to* them
- make sure that the way that you do it with them is:
  - whole-hearted
  - consistent.

Just doing that when it suits you is not enough. Nor is limiting what you trust them with. These will not work. You're going to have to take risks, throw away the key to your filing cabinet, open your files and let go of your 'authority'. You're going to have to learn to tolerate challenges – particularly to the old ways of doing things – and find ways of working together that foster and encourage creativity and new ideas.

Doing this and doing it well will be an act of courage – on your part. But it's not courage that's based on blind faith. For later in the week – on Monday – you'll be looking at the ways and means that you can use to do it. But remember this isn't a 'them and you' situation, it's an 'us' one. You're also involved.

Quality

Getting the quality of products and services right has become one of those 'must-do' issues. The change that's created this situation has involved everybody. As a consumer you expect your mail to be delivered quickly, the goods that you buy to be fit for their purpose and the meals that you buy in restaurants to be cooked and served in a manner which reflects the price you pay. If they're not, you complain.

In the increasingly competitive market places of the twenty-first century, no organization can assume that quality will happen on its own. Quality needs to be built into the system, managed, made certain. But that's not all that's needed. If quality is to contribute to the success of your performance management, it needs also to be about customer satisfaction. You'll look at this and how you can use it in more detail on Tuesday.

Measuring and monitoring

You measure things – or put a size, dimension or number to them – all the time. You measure your life span in years, months and days, your travel in miles or kilometres, your food in pounds, ounces or kilogrammes, your milk, beer or wine in quarts, pints or litres. Your car's performance is measured by its miles per gallon or kilometres per litre and your favourite baseball or soccer team's performance by the number of matches it wins or the number of goals it scores.

In your workplace, measurement is just as regular and commonplace an activity. If you make things, you measure and monitor the hours worked by your people, the output of your team, the costs and quantities of the raw materials used and the levels of scrap produced. If you work in a service organization, you measure and monitor the number of customers that you serve, the costs of doing that and how much money these customers spend on your particular service. But, almost all of these – the traditional measures of your workplace – :

- look inward rather than outward
- have short term, rather than long term, points of view
- are about money.

If you're going to be successful in your performance management then you'll need to take a wider view of what's going on. Instead of bean-counting, you need to make sure that the factors you measure and monitor are tuned to your organization's game plan. You'll also need to make sure that these are focused on and connected with answering your customer's needs. On Wednesday you'll take a look at the what, how and when of the sort of performance measuring and monitoring that does just that.

Goals, targets and benchmarks

We all have goals and targets. Yours may be about saving money, stopping smoking , losing weight, being tidier, getting a promotion or earning more money. Most of these are:

- expressed in general rather than specific terms
- concerned with long-term time scales
- about substantial changes .

The goals and targets of successful performance management are very different. For they are:

- specific and quantified
- easy to understand
- about continuous and ongoing activity
- concerned with results now – rather than tomorrow or next week.

Benchmarks can be used to help you to set up your goals and standards. These are measured standards which represent 'best practice' for some task or activity. You'll see on Thursday how these benchmarks can help you to set up realistic goals and targets for your performance management.

Techniques and tools

A technique, so the dictionary says, is a 'skilful or efficient means of achieving a purpose.' A technique is also a tool, a tool that you use to help you to achieve success in your performance management. The range and nature of these tools and the sort of uses that you put them to can be considerable. You can use them, for example, to:

- sort out what's happening
  - *input/output diagrams, flow charts, influence and multiple cause diagrams*
- solve problems
  - *lateral thinking, brainstorming, nominal group technique and Ishikawa diagrams*
- analyse data
  - *Pareto analysis, moving averages and cumulative sum plots*
- take decisions
  - *decision trees and fault analysis.*

In a book of this size, it's not possible to look at all of these techniques. So, on Thursday, you'll take a introductory look at a number of techniques that:

- are easy to learn and use
- will make a significant contribution to the success of your performance management.

But, as is so with all tools, the results that you achieve will depend upon *your* skill in their use.

When do you start?

The realisation that that you need to change the way that you do things can come to you in many ways. It can come when you catch a glimpse of a competitor's factory or office – and see that they do things differently – and better – than you do, when you see a programme on the TV or read a book that shows other alternatives. It can come as a result of days, weeks, months or years of dogged effort – aimed at trying to get the old way of doing things to work – and the growing realisation that that isn't going to happen. It can come like a flash of lightening – a sudden 'eureka!' experience that gives you the answer to the problem that's been bugging you for months, even years. There isn't a right or a wrong time to realise that you need to start your journey towards successful performance management – all of these are just as good as each other.

But start you must – and once you've done that, there will be no going back. Successful performance management isn't something that you can pick up – or drop – as and when you feel like it. Once you start your performance management you're in it for the long haul. It's an on-going commitment, a 24/7 lived-in process. If your performance management is going to be successful, it's got to be continuous and on-and-on – rather than one shot and on-and-off. But that's not all it's got to be – as you'll see when you look at the following ten commandments of successful performance management.

The ten commandments

Here, in preparation for the rest of your week, are the' ten commandments' of successful performance management.

1 Successful performance management is no longer an optional extra.
2 Successful performance management means accepting and embracing change rather than holding it at arm's length.
3 Successful performance management is a continuous and on-going process, rather than a one-off project.
4 Performance management is a 'people centred' activity.
5 Successful performance management is done *with* people, not *to* them.
6 Successful performance management is driven by the gap between where you are now and where you want to be.
7 Successful performance management measures are credible and understandable.
8 Successful performance management measures are about efficiency, effectiveness and adaptability.
9 Successful performance management uses techniques that are relevant and effective – and uses them well.
10 The ultimate judge of your performance management is the customer – and they deserve to be delighted.

People and successful performance management

Yesterday you looked at the what, why, when and how of successful performance management. You saw that the drivers of this process are:

- People
- Quality
- Measuring and monitoring
- Goals, targets and benchmarks
- Techniques and tools

Now, on Monday, you're going to look at the first of these – people – and when you've done that you'll have looked at:

- Shifting up to doing it *with* people, rather than *to* them
- Change – and managing it
- Motivation
- Workplace needs
- Working together to solve problems
- Working ways – in teams and projects
- Training for skills and knowledge

Shifting up

People are core to the process of successful performance management.

If your performance management is going to be successful,
you've got to tap into the 'creative spark' that comes from
people. This means that you've got to do your performance
management *with* people – rather than *to* them. Doing this
will probably mean an attitude shift on your part; a shift
that'll take you to where you begin to see that these people
are:

- creative individuals – rather than just paid
  employees who do only what they are told to do
- a vital part of the solution, rather than 'the problem'
- key parts of a formidable team – with you – rather
  than solo players.

Making this shift, and doing it well, will be an act of courage
on your part.

'Change yourself, change your fortunes.'
Portuguese proverb

It will change the way you do your job. You'll find yourself
involving them when you take decisions – not just when it
suits you. You'll find yourself taking risks with them, opening
your files to them, letting go of your 'authority'. You'll find
yourself doing less 'managing' and more 'co-ordinating.'
You'll also need to find (and use) new ways of working
with them.

New ways

Changing the ways that you work with the people of your workplace is not an easy option. It will take time, patience and commitment to make the shift that is needed in this key element of your performance management. On the way, there will be upsets, setbacks, conflicts and compromises. But doing it – making that shift – *is* worth the trouble that's involved. For once it is made you'll be able to drop the old ways of people management – based on threats, manipulation and domination – and pick up the new twenty-first century ways – based on sharing, co-operation and consensus. Doing this isn't just important – it is also realistic. For it recognises that we live in a changing world – one in which educational backgrounds, needs, desires and attitudes to work have changed. So finding new ways of managing people is not just important – it is *essential*. But first you need to look at change itself and how you can manage it.

Change

Change, as somebody once said, is the window through which the future enters your life. It's all around you, all of the time, and its variety is incredible. It can be large or small, short-lived or drawn out, one-off or repetitive, periodic or continuous, permanent or reversible. You can bring it about yourself or it can come in ways that give you no choice about its when, what or how. Most people don't like change – or rather, they don't like being changed. When change looms, fear and resistance follow. We fight against change – despite its sometimes obvious benefits. We do this for a number of reasons, including that we:

- fear the loss of something that we value, or
- don't understood the change and its implications, or
- don't think that the change makes sense, or
- find it difficult to cope with either the level or pace of the change.

Fighting change can slow it down, even divert it, but it won't stop it. If your performance management is going to be successful, you must learn to look on change as a friend – one who presents you with an opportunity for growth and improvement. So how can you do this? Part of the answer lies in your own experience. After all, you've been surrounded by change all your life – and have survived to tell the tale. There will have been circumstances where you've fought against change and other circumstances where you've accepted it willingly and with enthusiasm. When you've accepted change it was usually because you believed that what was to come

was more attractive and interesting than what you had. This
gives you a clue to how you can manage change successfully.

Managing change

If you're going to manage change effectively, you need to be
aware that the way that people behave is a bit of a balancing
act. What are balanced are the forces that act upon us. Some
of these are trying to get us to change our behaviour and
others are trying to restrain or limit that change. This
balancing act goes on all the time and is influenced by the
people around you. If you want to create a change, you must
either:

- increase or strengthen one or all of the forces for
  change, or
- reduce or weaken one or all of the restraining forces.

Either of these will cause a shift or change. A new balance is
then established. Doing that involves the following steps:

1 Identify the change that you want to achieve.
2 List the forces that:
   - will help you to achieve that change
   - will hinder that change.
3 Decide:
   - which of these you're going to strengthen or
     weaken
   - how you're going to do that
   - when you're going to do it.
4 Do it.

Getting this right – managing change well – is a skill that can make a major contribution to your performance management. What you need to do now is to look at some of the forces – or needs and motives – that act upon us all.

Motivation

A lot has been written about motives and motivation, most of it aimed at answering questions like 'Why do people come to work?' But for you, now, the question that needs to be answered is 'How can I help them to improve their performance while they are here?' You'll notice that 'help' is used – rather than 'manage' or 'direct' or 'control'. If you doubt the wisdom of this, take at look at the sort of things that your people do when they are not at work. You'll probably find the range of these is considerable – singing in a choir, running a troop of scouts, studying for a qualification, building model 'planes, learning to play the piano, breeding stick insects. They do these because they want to, rather than to earn money, and they do them in ways that are self managed, creative and energetic, rather than 'by the book'. The challenge that you face is how to get all of that 'can-do' stuff into your workplace.

Most of us do the things that we do because we think that they'll lead to us getting something that we want or need. One view of these 'wants and needs' divides them into groups that can be arranged or 'stacked', one above another, as on a staircase. On the first, and lowest, step are our physical needs – food, warmth and shelter. Above these in turn are our needs for:

- protection and security
- affection and attachment
- reputation and recognition, and, at the top,
- self-fulfilment.

We act in ways that aim to get these needs answered in their order on the 'staircase'. For example, we satisfy our basic need for warmth, food, water and shelter before we begin to seek answers to our 'higher' needs, such as job security, prestige and the freedom to create.

Workplace needs

When you transfer all of this into the workplace, some important ideas begin to emerge. These tell you that people don't just come to work for the money. They want to achieve. They want to work toward targets that are meaningful. They have more potential than you think they have and they're capable of accepting more responsibility than you've given them so far. All of this tells you that people work best in a workplace that allows them to direct and control their own efforts towards goals that they've been involved in defining.

To get this to happen you need to:

- work with them to identify tasks that are meaningful to them
- find ways of working together that create solutions, rather than problems
- match individuals to tasks
- make sure they have the skills, knowledge and information they need

Working together to solve problems

Houston, we have a problem

When you start to work with people in this way, it won't be easy. There'll be problems. You'll have difficulties and you'll get awkward situations. But not all of these will be as serious – or as obvious – as the one that faced the crew of Apollo 11. Often you'll have to work hard to find out exactly what's happening. Later in the week (Friday) you'll look at techniques that will help you – and the people you're working with – to do just that. Now, at this point in your week, you need to look at how to identify the benefit – for everybody – that solving a problem generates.

Creativity is not a separate part of thinking

Edward de Bono

Problems, benefits and solutions

Let's look at a simple, but common, problem – car parking. These days, most people own a car and use it to get to work. When they get there there's often limited space for parking and they have to spend time, driving round, trying to find somewhere to park. As a consequence, they're late for work, they're annoyed and upset. The old-fashioned solution to the parking space problem is to ration out and control the parking space you've got. Typically, you'll mark out or reserve spaces for the managers and let everybody else take pot luck. But doing that only serves to highlight the differences between you and them, rather than the interests that you have in common.

In your new way of working, you'll start working together by identifying:

- the benefits you'll share when you solve the problem
- the alternative ways of doing it.

This way, you'll look at car-clubs, busing, parking rotas, who gets a reserved space and extending the car park with reserved spots for everybody. You'll do that together and when you do it you'll look at all the implications – including their cost. If you do it right, you'll *all* see where the most benefit lies and which solution contributes most to everybody's economic well-being. It's a 'can-do' way of solving problems that taps into everyone's abilities and creativity. But to do this, and do it successfully, you've got to be able to communicate well. Doing this isn't just about telling people what you think – it's also about listening to what they say. You've got to allow time for this to happen, for people to build up enough trust in you to tell you what they think. Let's take a look at two of the ways that will help you to achieve that working together.

Working ways – teams and projects

Teams
'Team' is one of those words that we use a lot – usually to describe the squads of people who play sports such as soccer or baseball. But we also have teams in our workplaces. We have sales teams, assembly teams, clean-up teams, problem solving teams, management teams – and more ! This is because the team, in all of these guises, is a device or mechanism that enables you to:

- tap into the skills, abilities and creativity of all the people in it
- use all of those to greater effect in the workplace.

When you use teams in your performance management, they will give you the potential to:

- make things happen – quicker and better
- create solutions to problems
- find ways of moving your performance management up a gear.

All of this happens because the team acts like a lens – as you can see below:

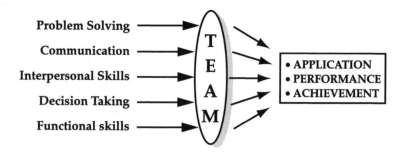

Projects

One of the ways you can use your teams is in your performance management projects. Yesterday you saw that successful performance management is a continuous and on-going process made up of small, subtle increments, rather than big jumps. It's also low cost and do-it-on-the-budget actions, rather than capital-hungry. A project is one of the tools that help you achieve all of that. It's a tool with a track record of creating success and using that to build further success. It looks for results *now*, rather than some vague tomorrow that never quite arrives. But performance management projects are *special*. They involve limited capital spend and have goals that are achievable in the short term. They also involve people – in teams that empower rather than limit or control. These are the teams that make things happen. But working in these and the other teams of your performance management will demand a wider range of different skills from your people. To answer these demands they'll need training.

THIS IS WHERE WE
FELL OFF THE CRITICAL
PATH...

Training for skills and knowledge

Skills and knowledge are essential to the success of your performance management. The best way of making sure that your people get the skills and knowledge that *they* need is to train them. Training and learning go hand in hand – or , at least, they *ought* to. If you get them right you'll change, often permanently, both what's done and the way it's done. But training has to have a focus or a purpose. It should be aimed at answering individual, rather than general, needs. You'll find out what these needs are and answer them by taking the following five steps. Try them on yourself first – after all, you may also need some new skills!

1 Identify current skills
   Be both realistic and accurate. Don't claim skills or knowledge that aren't there. Do include skills that have been learnt and used outside the workplace.
2 Identify the skills that the task, project or new situation demands. Again, be as realistic and specific as you can.
3 The skill gap
   Compare what you found in Steps 1 and 2 – this is the skill gap. Set down goals and priorities. Which comes first – learning about computers or learning bookkeeping? Generate a training plan.
4 Check out
   Get someone else to check out your training plan. Remember you won't have got it all right and you may need to accept some changes to your plan.
5 Doing it
   Choosing the right training course is rather like choosing a good builder – personal recommendation works best. Ask around, find people who've been on courses like the ones that you're interested in. See what they say about how and if it worked for them.

Summary

Today, you have looked at the first of the agents of successful performance management, people. In the days that follow, you'll be looking at the others – quality, goals, targets and plans, measures and benchmarks and techniques. Here's a summary of Monday:

- People are core to successful performance management.
- Successful performance management is done *with* people rather than *to* them.
- Do this, and do it well, and you'll need to:
  - manage change effectively
  - tap into people's creativity and energy
  - solve problems with solutions that benefit everybody.
- Teams and projects will help you to do that.
- Teams make things happen quicker and better and find ways of moving your performance management up a gear.
- The project is one of the tools that can help you achieve success in your performance management.
- To achieve success in your performance management you and your people will need more and different skills.
- Training can give you these skills, provided it's based on an accurate and honest assessment of what you need.

Quality and successful performance management

Today you'll look at the second of the drivers of successful performance management – quality. When you do that, you'll find that quality can – if you manage it well – make a major contribution to the success of your performance management.

By the end of this day you'll have looked at the following:

- What do we mean by quality?
- Twenty-first century quality
- The steps to quality
- Customers
- Total quality
- Quality assurance
- Common fallacies about quality
- Getting it right
- The quality gurus

What do we mean by quality?

Quality is one of those words that we all use – and misuse – a lot. We talk about things like 'quality' cars or spending 'quality' time with our children. It's a commonly used word. But are these sorts of 'quality' the same as the quality that drives your successful performance management – or is that different? When you look the word 'quality' up in a dictionary, you'll find a definition that tells you it's 'the degree of goodness or value'. But none of these are correct when it comes to the quality in your performance management. For this quality is different. It's not about worth or value. It's about answering needs, purpose and use.

'Quality has to be defined as conformance to requirements, not as goodness.'

Philip Crosby

'Quality is fitness for purpose or use.'

Joseph Juran

What this tells you is that anything can possess quality, providing that:

- its purpose is adequately and clearly defined
- its performance meets that definition.

This means that a paper tissue is as much a quality product as a silk handkerchief and a Citroen 2CV as a Rolls Royce. Each of these has a different purpose but they all demonstrate 'fitness for purpose' and hence, quality.

Twenty-first century quality

So how does quality rate at the beginning of the twenty-first century? The answer is simple: it is no longer an optional extra. Quality has become an essential element in all organizational 'tool boxes'. Today's business environment is volatile, challenging and fast; organizational survival demands agility, adaptability and, above all, the ability to respond to customer needs. Twenty-first century quality means doing just that – answering customer needs – and responding to their rising expectations about the reliability, value and durability of the goods and services that you provide.

So how did this happen, why have organizations shifted away from the old 'take-it-or-leave-it' attitude towards customers? The answer lies back in the early 1950s – with the Japanese manufacturing industry. At that time Japan needed to import almost all its raw materials – at considerable cost. As a result, industry began to exploit and develop techniques aimed at producing quality goods with lower production costs. These included 'just-in-time' (JIT) scheduling, quality tools like the 'Fishbone' diagram and statistical quality control methods such as the Shewart chart. In time, these came together in an integrated approach – Total Quality Management (TQM). The results were impressive, significant and obvious. 'Getting it right first time' and 'delighting' customers by anticipating their needs became the management mantras that spread across the manufacturing industries of the world. As you will see shortly, TQM is a very powerful tool in the contest to achieve survival and success. But before you do that let's look at some of the basics of twenty-first century quality.

The steps to quality

You've already seen that a quality product or service has its roots deep in its defined purpose. That purpose or list of performance requirements is often called its specification. This can be used to identify the characteristics of both what the product or service does – its functionality – and its non-functional characteristics, such as how it is styled or appears. Both of these are important. But that specification must meet and reflect the needs of the customer. These are the steps that will make sure that you do that:

1 Identify the customer need
2 Decide which part of that need will be answered by the product or service
3 Detail key characteristics or performance of the service or product to answer that part of the need
4 Design that product or service taking into account both the customer need and the capabilities of the organization
5 Create that product or service that ensures that it meets customer needs and is in response to an evident or anticipated customer demand.

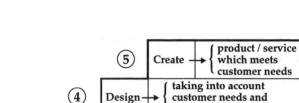

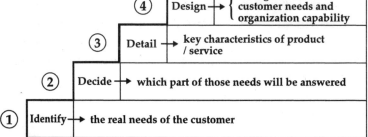

⑤	Create →	product / service which meets customer needs
④	Design →	taking into account customer needs and organization capability
③	Detail →	key characteristics of product / service
②	Decide →	which part of those needs will be answered
①	Identify →	the real needs of the customer

Customers

Customers are important. After all, they are the people (and organizations) who buy the products and services that you design, create, support or sell in your workplace. But don't make the mistake of thinking that these people – the outside or *external* customers – are the only ones with an interest in those products or services. In fact, your workplace is full of customers. These are the people who work down the corridor, in the next office, at the next desk, over at the Newark plant. They are the people for whom you fill in a form, complete your monthly returns, complete a design, write a report. They are your *internal* customers.

This idea of the internal customer is a far-reaching one. For if, in your workplace, you're not serving the external customer, then you must be serving someone who is. The quality of the service that you provide to that 'someone' – that internal customer – will have a direct effect upon the nature of the service that they can provide to the external customer. This means that 'getting it right' for the internal customer is a vital link in the chain of actions that leads to success with your external customer. But getting the balance right is also important. Meeting – even exceeding – the expectations of your external customer must come first. Forget that – and become myopically 'locked into' your internal processes – and you run the risk of losing that external customer. A key step towards successful performance management is to make sure that the needs of your internal customers are focused on satisfying the external customer – and that they are met.

Total quality

You can take these ideas – of the internal/external customer and the chain of inter-linked steps or actions that lead to success with your external customer – further when you look at the idea of total quality management or TQM. This is:

- *total* because it's about everything that contributes to the final product or service and everybody who's involved in it
- about *quality* as in 'fitness for purpose'
- concerned with *management*, because it's a process that's managed rather than an 'add-on' extra.

But TQM isn't just a way of managing quality. It is, in fact, a way of managing organizations. Getting all of this right – making sure that everyone in the 'quality chain' has got it right – isn't easy. But if you want to know more about TQM there's another book in this series that will help you – *Total Quality Management in a week.*

Quality assurance

Quality assurance (QA) systems are about giving management 'adequate confidence that a product or service will satisfy given requirements for quality'. Companies use QA systems to demonstrate to their customers that their quality needs are of prime importance. As such, these systems can be seen as a way of keeping your existing customers and growing with your new ones. The commonest sort of QA systems are those based on the International Series of Standards (ISO). These are quite detailed and to conform to them you'll need to be sure that, amongst other things, your:

- raw materials and services conform to specified requirements
- product meets its specification
- people know how to do their jobs – and are trained to do them
- off-spec material is identified and segregated.

Despite the power and value of these quality assurance systems, they are not enough on their own. But, as part of a TQM process, they can lead to 'delighted' customers as well as being a key active agent in your performance management.

Common fallacies about quality

There are lots of fallacies about quality. Here are some of the most common:

Quality cannot be measured
This assumes that quality is intangible and cannot be measured. But quality can be measured by looking at how much it costs to ensure conformance – even if some parts of the customer requirement or specification are intangible or aesthetic !

Quality = high cost or value
This use of the word 'quality' reflects the value or price of the goods – rather than their functionality. But an expensive car can only be a quality car if it satisfies the requirements of the customer. However, other customers may have more modest needs that are fulfilled by a smaller, more modest vehicle. But this also is a quality car – because it satisfies customer requirements.

Quality Control Departments generate quality
Quality Control Departments don't create quality – they are only concerned with its measurement or identification. It takes a lot more than the presence of a Quality Control Department to create a quality organization.

Quality improvement costs money rather than making profit
The Japanese were the first to prove that quality

improvement generates benefits in terms of productivity, market share etc. As such it's a benefit generator rather than a 'cost sink'.

Quality problems originate with people at the 'sharp end'
While most quality problems surface at the 'sharp end' – on the shop floor, over the counter or at the reception desk – their roots and origins are often further back – in design, accounting, purchasing or marketing.

Getting it right

Bringing quality to its full potential as a performance management driver isn't easy. It takes commitment, the willingness to change and hard work to get TQM up and running successfully. You've probably heard of companies who tried – and failed – to get TQM integrated with the other drivers of their performance management and finished up disappointed. If you're going to avoid this happening to you here are some of the things that you shouldn't and should do:

You should not:	You should:
Look for a quick fix	Be there for the long haul
Lack management commitment	All be committed
Exclude people	Involve everyone
Lack vision	See where you're going – and why

Get stuck in bureaucracy or gimmicky tools	Get and stay open, cool and focused
Resist change	Embrace change
Lack measurables to monitor your progress	Set up measurables that are cheap, understandable and easy – and use them

The quality gurus

W Edwards Deming
Deming's methods of statistical quality control were taken up with enthusiasm by Japanese engineers and managers. The success of these led to the establishment, in 1951, of the Deming prize for contributions to quality and the award to Deming, in 1960, of Japan's premier Imperial honour, the Second Order of the Sacred Treasure. Deming's subsequent work moved on to a more management-based approach with 14 key points and a seven point action plan ('Out of Crisis', 1982).

Joseph M Juran
Juran is often credited with converting the influence upon the Japanese of statistical control-led Deming approach into a broader concern with the management of quality. He published 12 books which have been translated into some 13 languages and has received more than 30 medals and awards in various countries. His 'Quality Planning Road Map' has nine steps and believes that the majority of quality problems are due to poor management.

Shigeo Shingo

Shingo extended the ideas of quality control to develop the 'Poka – Yoke', mistake proofing or 'Defects = 0' concepts – all of which were applied with great success. He published 14 or more books which have been translated into English and other European languages.

Philip B Crosby

An American who is best known for the concepts of 'Do It Right First Time' and 'Zero Defects', Crosby put forward four absolutes of quality: quality = conformance to requirements, quality comes from prevention and 'right first time', cost is the measure of quality and zero defects as the standard of performance. These were used as the basis of a 14 point quality improvement plan. Books published include 'Quality is Free', 'Quality without Tears' and 'The Art of Getting Your Own Sweet Way'.

Armand V Feigenbaum

Feigenbaum was head of quality at GEC and his book 'Quality Control: Principles, Practices and Administration' argued for a move away from the technology of quality control towards the use of quality control as a business method. Other major themes were the cost of quality, the need for a 'right first time' attitude and the need for everyone to be responsible for quality.

Kaoru Ishikawa

A leader in Japan's quality movement, Ishikawa paid particular attention to both techniques (Pareto, cause and effect diagrams, scatter diagrams, Shewart control charts etc) and organizational approaches (quality circles, company wide quality control) .

Genichi Taguchi

Taguchi developed the 'quality loss function' concept in which quality and reliability are established in the design phase and the routine optimisation of the product and plant prior to manufacture – instead of being reliant upon quality through inspection.

Walter A. Shewart

A researcher at Bell Laboratories. Shewart was a pioneer of the use and development of quality control. He published two books (*Economic Control of Quality of Manufactured Product, Statistical Method from the Viewpoint of Quality Control*) and created the 'plan-do-check-act' (PDCA) cycle. He also introduced the use of control charts and the idea that quality could be 'objective' and independent or 'subjective' and perceived.

Claus Moller

A Danish economist whose company (Time Manager International) has developed a number of management training programmes. Moller sees personal quality as the basis of all other types of quality and in his book *Personal Quality* identifies two standards of personal quality: the ideal performance level (IP) and the actual performance level (AP). He identifies the twelve 'Golden Rules' that help improve the AP level and describes the seventeen hallmarks of a quality company.

Summary

Today, you have looked at the second of the agents of successful performance management – quality. Tomorrow you'll be looking at the next of these agents, measuring and monitoring, and in the days that follow you'll look at goals, targets and benchmarks and techniques.

Here's a summary of Tuesday:

- Quality = fitness for purpose or use.
- Anything can possess quality providing its purpose is clearly defined and its performance meets that definition.
- The steps to quality involve identifying customer need, deciding which part of that need you're going to answer, detailing the answer to that need and designing and creating the answer.
- Internal and external customers are both important.

- Total quality management (TQM) is a way of managing organizations.
- Quality assurance (QA) systems are about delighting your customer – consistently.
- Most common fallacies about quality don't stand up to examination.
- Getting it right means being there for the long haul and involving everyone as well as embracing change, having a vision of where you're going and using measurables to monitor your progress.
- Most quality gurus tell us that it's the management of quality that's important – rather than its control.

Measurement and monitoring for successful performance management

This is the day that you'll look at the ways, means and focus of the measuring and monitoring of your successful performance management. When you've done that you'll have looked at:

- Measuring your performance
- What you should measure
- Efficiency
- Effectiveness
- Adaptability
- Where, when and who
- Monitoring
- Planning and setting up your system

Measuring your performance

Getting your performance measurement right is important. If you can do that, the data you generate will tell you where you are. It will also tell you – when compared to standards or records – how you are doing. All of this gives you feedback. This feedback will tell you whether you are – or aren't:

- doing the right things
- doing them well.

But that's not all that performance measurement will give you. It will also provide the motivation that will spur you on to improve your performance. It will provide the incentive for you to 'do it better.'

But for all of this to happen you must make sure that you measure the 'right' things at the 'right' time and in the 'right' place. These measures must also – since they're going to be with you in the long run – be tuned in to the 'game plan ' of your organization or business unit.

What you should measure

You can measure your performance in a number of ways. If you are an estate agent, for example, you can count the number of potential client contacts you have each day or the average daily fee revenue that you earn or the proportion of your contacts that get converted into sales. Each of these is important and each of them reflects a different aspect of your business. In most organizations the performance measures available are just as varied. But those that get chosen are often focused on the short, rather than the long, term and are generated by complex accounting systems. They often appear too late or are too remote from the 'coal-face' and they are complicated and expensive to produce. Above all, they are remote from customer satisfaction.

The performance measures that you choose – whatever they are about – must be:

- easily understood and generated
- inexpensive to measure and near to the 'action'
- motivating and directly related to customer satisfaction.

But that's not all they must be. For these measures must also be accessible and credible. They must respond to the actions of your people, rather than the whims and eccentricities of the $/£ exchange rate. To do that they are going to focus on the following:

- the efficiency of your business unit
- its effectiveness
- its adaptability.

Efficiency

Efficiency is about the way you use your resources. In its simplest form efficiency is expressed as:

Efficiency = Output/Input

An efficiency measure for your car is its miles per gallon or kilometres per litre of fuel. The figure you achieve for this and the way it varies tells you about not just the efficiency of the engine but also:

- the effect of your driving style
- the condition of the engine
- the effect of route or journey.

In the workplace, your efficiency measure can take a variety of forms and here are some examples

Productivity measure: Work done per person per hour

Time measure: Average time taken to process a
              planning application

Service volume measure: Number of repairs
                        undertaken per day

Cost measure: Energy cost per square metre
              of floor-space

But these efficiency ratios are only concerned with resource utilisation. They are not concerned with whether the service or product generated is relevant and available when and where the customer needs it.

Effectiveness

Effectiveness takes you beyond efficiency. When what you do is effective, it meets the needs of both the internal and external customers. While efficiency is about how well you use your resources, effectiveness is concerned with how well you provide the 'right' service at the 'right' place and the 'right' time. An efficient shop assistant will serve a high number of customers per hour. But the effective shop assistant aims at long-term revenue generation by spending more time satisfying customer's needs and hence achieving higher levels of customer repeat and referral business. An effective shop assistant's customers come back to buy again and tell their friends how good a service they were given. Here are some other examples of effectiveness:

Role task	Efficiency measure	Effectiveness measure
Newspaper reporter	Reporter hours per story	% stories printed in paper
College lecturer	Number of hours taught	% student pass rate
	Students per class	% students with job
	Number of publications	offers at end of course
Shop assistant	Customers served per hour	Average sale per customer
Reservations clerk	Minutes per call	% calls leading to booking
Lathe operator	Parts completed per hour	% accepted parts per hour
Secretary	Letters typed per hour	% correct letters sent out

These examples of effectiveness measures tell you that the needs of the customer can sometimes override your efficiency needs. You need to be able to balance efficiency needs with your need for customer effectiveness.

Adaptability

Measures that tell you about your efficiency or effectiveness aren't all that you need. You also need to be adaptable if you're really going to answer the needs of your customers. Being adaptable means being able to adjust, fit or change your products and services so that they meet *any* customer need. It's adaptability that gives us the legends of good customer service. These are the hotels that remember and answer your special idiosyncratic needs, the airlines that hold flights open until the last minute because of heavy traffic or bad weather on the road from town and the department stores that alter an off-the-peg suit in time for a next-day wedding.

Adaptability measures
- Number of customer complaints about lack of adaptability of standard service or product
- Comparison between average response time or processing time for standard and for special services or products
- % of special requests referred upwards in organization
- % special requests

When, where and who

When
Once you've decided what aspect of your business unit is
going to be the focus of your performance measurement
system there's another decision to take. For now you have to
decide how often you're going to measure it. This can have
quite an influence on:

- the way you respond to what you've measured
- how effective that response is.

Long periods between measurements can lead to
inappropriate and out-of-date responses, allowing problems
to continue and increase. Short periods can lead to over-
reaction, cause instability, 'hunting' and cycling. What the
'right' frequency is for your measurements will be a matter of
trial and error and, finally, of judgement on your part. But
before you make that judgement, make sure that the
measurement:

- takes place at a frequency that reflects the speed that things around you are changing,
- is compatible with your existing reporting systems.

Where

Most traditional performance measurement systems measure performance by locking on to what comes out at the end. But the information that this gives you is of limited value. It doesn't tell you much about the individual activities that go on inside the work place and what it does tell you is also out-of-date. If your performance measurement is going to be any use at all, it must take place at points that are close to each of the activities of your unit. This will give you information that's timely and focused and provide direct and immediate feedback to the people involved in that activity. Mapping out the workflow of your unit will help you to identify these points – it may also surprise you to see what goes where!

Who

There are two bites to the 'Who' of your performance measuring and monitoring.

- Who is measured?
- Who does the measuring?

You already have the answer to the first of these. You know that your measurements should take place as close as you can manage to each of the activities that take place in your business unit. This means that the 'who' that are measured are the people who undertake each of these activities. When you move onto the next question – who does the measurement? – it's the same answer: the people who undertake each of these activities. If you think about it, you'll soon realise that these are the only answers that make any sense. For your successful performance management is being done *with* these people, not *to* them. You'll need to accept that those who do it can also measure and monitor how well they are doing it. This shift to 'self inspection' or 'self-monitoring' is important. It involves:

- trust – you have to trust that they will do it and do it when it needs doing
- training – you have to show them how to do it
- empowerment – they decide what to do about it and may even decide what to measure.

Training and time will be needed for this measurement and monitoring. You'll also need analytical techniques. On Friday you'll meet some of these, such as moving average and CUSUM, that can help here. Why don't you start by asking people what they think ought to be measured and monitored!

Monitoring

Monitoring, the dictionary tells us, is about 'observing, supervising or keeping under control.' First, you measure something, then you monitor it. But if you're going to monitor your performance well, your measurements need to be more than just accurate. They also need to be reliable, economic and repeatable. The data that they generate can then be recorded and organised in such a way that you can:

- compare week with week, month with month or year with year
- analyse them – so that you can find out about long-term trends, patterns or other effects.

But this isn't just passive data that you're recording. It's active, it can give you the answers to questions such as 'Am I on schedule?' or 'Have I overspent the budget?' But that's not all that your monitoring will tell you. It will also tell you whether or not your business unit is drifting 'off-course', failing to perform as you need it to. If that's the signal it gives you, you can begin to do something about it – and bring its performance back 'on course.' To do this, your monitoring has to focus on key areas, rather than be an indiscriminate across-the-board activity. Your performance measurement and monitoring needs to be focused on to the 'pulse–points' of your business unit. This sort of regular monitoring keeps you in touch with what's happening.

Planning and setting up your system

Let's assume that by now you've decided the what, where, when and who of your performance management measurement. If you're sensible, you'll have done this with a small working party or team of your people. You'll have gone on with that team to work out the detail of your performance monitoring. So is that all you need to do? The answer is no – now you've got to:

- make sure that everybody in your business unit understands the what and why of your system
- provide enough appropriate support and resources
- set up and run a limited span pilot run of at least three months duration
- hand-pick the people involved
- empower those people – so that they can get results.

Getting your measuring and monitoring system up and running and giving you the data that you need takes time, patience and perseverance – and that takes planning.

Planning

But this won't be just any old back-of-an-envelope plan. It will need to be a plan that's effective, a plan that will get your system up and running in the shortest possible time and at minimum cost. Creating and using a plan like this takes real skill. It needs to be a plan that's:

- flexible and able to cope with change
- clear and specific in its content
- easily understood by all who use or see it.

When you create a plan like this it'll also:

- provide a starting point for common understanding and co-operative effort
- be a way telling people about what's going on.

Your plan must be simple enough to be understood by people with little or no experience of plans or planning – so that you can use it to sell the idea of performance management to everybody. Start by listing what you need to do in order to set up your performance measurement and monitoring system. Remember that your motto is 'start small and grow'. It's neither necessary nor sensible for you to begin by covering your whole operation.

Setting up
Setting up your measuring and monitoring system and getting it to work effectively and well takes quite a lot of time and effort. It also takes the co-operation and support of the people that you work with. Whatever your plans might be, it's those people who actually do it. It's their ability to make this system work, to overcome its initial problems, that will make the difference between success and failure. Here are the key steps towards doing that:

- start on a small scale
- get rid of the snags and bugs
- demonstrate tangible benefits

Summary

Today you've looked at the sort of measuring and monitoring that will lead to your successful performance management. Tomorrow you'll be looking at how you can use that information to create the goals and targets of your successful performance management and whether benchmarks can help you to do that. Here's a summary of Wednesday:

- Measures give you feedback and need to be:
  - easily understood
  - easily generated
  - inexpensive to measure
  - near to the 'action'
  - motivating
  - directly related to customer satisfaction.
- Measures also need to be accessible and credible.
- Measurement systems can focus on:
  - efficiency – or resource utilisation
  - effectiveness – whether you give your customer the 'right' service at the 'right' place and time
  - adaptability – really answering the needs of your customers.
- The 'when', 'where' and 'who' of your measurement system are key to its effectiveness.
- Monitor your measures, analyse the information and use it to keep your business unit on course.
- Plan the how and when of your measurement and monitoring.
- Start small and grow.

Goals, targets and benchmarks for successful performance management

Today you'll move on to look at what you can do with the results of your performance measurement and monitoring and how you can use them to identify and achieve the goals, targets and benchmarks of your successful performance management. When you've done that you'll have looked at:

- What's next?
- What gap?
- Cause and Effect
- Options – identifying and choosing
- Test and trial
- Review and modify
- Implementation
- The next step
- Benchmarks and benchmarking

What's next?

You've got your pilot measurement and monitoring scheme up and running, you've sorted the bugs out, the data's coming in and everybody's happy. So what happens now, what comes next? The answer is that now you're going to have to do something with this data, something that will move you – in performance terms – from where you are to where you want to be.

To do this, you're going to have to take the following steps:

- identify the gap between where you are and where you want to be
- find the causes of that gap
- look at options for closing that gap
- select one for trial or test
- implement that trial and review its results
- modify or reject the option as required
- implement that action.

Getting all of these right isn't just important – it's vital. For it can make the difference between success and failure in your performance management.

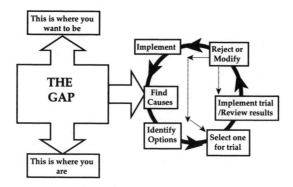

What gap?

Your performance measurement and monitoring tells you where you are. But that's not enough. If you're going to improve your performance, you'll need a target or goal to aim for. But this can't be just any old goal or target. It's worth reminding yourself of what you read on Sunday about this goal. You saw then that it must be:

- specific and quantified, rather than vague and generalised
- concerned with results *now*, rather than next week
- easily understandable, rather than complicated or jargonized
- achieved by continuous, on-going and incremental activity, rather than on-off chunks of major effort.

Your movement towards that goal will be fuelled by the gap between it and where you are now. Later this week – on Saturday – you'll also see that your goals and targets need to be compatible with the long-term view or strategy of your organization. But if your goals and targets and the gap between them and where you are now are going to be more than just notional flag-posts in some vague possible future, you'll need to:

- identify and choose those goals and targets with care
- plan, prepare for and implement with care and forethought the actions that you take in order to achieve them.

Achieving all this doesn't happen overnight. It will take time, effort and thought to get your efforts focused so that you bridge the gap between that target and where you are now. But that's not all that must happen. If your performance management is going to be successful, these goals and targets must be meaningful to those around you in your workplace. They must turn people on, set fire to their imaginations. In short, they must motivate them.

Cause and effect

You've set up your goals and targets and identified the gap between them and your current performance. Now you need to identify what it is that causes this gap. You need to find answers to questions such as 'Why does your performance move up and down?' or 'Why isn't your performance higher?' You can do this in a number of ways. You can do it by rigorous analysis or by less rigorous, but just as effective, 'creative' methods. You can do it in a team or on your own. On Friday you'll look at some of the techniques that you can use. Used well, these will point you towards whatever it is that's causing the gap between the performance that you've measured and monitored and where you want to be. Doing this takes patience, time and perseverance. But it isn't necessary to find out everything. Getting all the answers and over-analysing everything will only delay your performance improvement.

Options – identifying and choosing

You've identified what it is that's making your performance go up and down. Now you have to decide what the options are for what might be done about it. It's important to realise that what you're facing isn't a problem – it's an opportunity for change. It's one that can enable you to get rid of the old inefficient, ineffective and rigid ways of doing things and find new efficient, effective and adaptable ways. When you do that, it's important that you take off the old 'blinkers' – the ones that, in the past, have kept you from seeing solutions that seem too radical, revolutionary, or even too simple to work. Try using brainstorming, nominal group technique or visioning to generate your list of 'might-dos' and have the courage to include the 'wild-card' solutions. When you do that, you'll finish up with a list of options for reducing or eliminating the difference between where you are now and where you want to be. What you must now decide is which option you're going to use. The best way to do this is to choose those options which are:

- simplest, or
- most efficient, or
- most economical.

It's also worth adding those that are:

- most easily understood, or
- have most support.

Whichever one you choose you must, if that option is to succeed, take account of the views of those who will be involved in implementation and use.

Test and trial

The Russian revolutionary, Lenin, wrote that nations and people generally took 'one step forward and two steps back' in their search for improvement. In your search for success in your performance management, you'll start by taking a single small step forward – that of a trial or test of your chosen option. If this is going to succeed, it needs to be planned with care and monitored.

You also need to be aware that this test or trial may be seen, by others, as a challenge or threat – because it's a change. This means that you need to make sure that you tell everybody about what's happening – even if they're not directly involved.

Review and modify

At some point you're going to sit down and take a good hard look at the results that this trial is generating. When you do this is up to you. It can be after the trial has run for a certain period of time, at some arbitrary 'half-way point' or when you've passed a milestone. Make sure that the trial has run for an adequate period of time before you review it. Whatever you're doing differently has to have had enough time to settle in, get de-bugged and get exposed to a wide enough range of situations. When you get to that point, the questions that you'll be asking will be:

- did we achieve our targets?
- if not, why not?
- did we have the right type and quantity of resources?

The answers that you get will enable you to decide whether you:

- make the option permanent in its present form, or
- implement an extended or larger version, or
- modify and re-trial the option, or
- trial another option.

The last two of these will mean that you need to go back and either set up and run another trial or choose another option to trial. If, however, you decide to move forward to a permanent or large scale version of your trialed option, you need to make sure that everybody understands what you're doing and why you're doing it. Be careful how you do this , make sure that you don't slip back into the the old 'because I say so' routine. Make sure that you do whatever you do *with* rather than *to* the people of your business unit .

Implementation

Let's assume that your trial has been successful. Now you want to move forward, convert your gap-closing option into a permanent feature of your operation or apply it in other areas or on a bigger scale. The keywords here are, yet again, preparation, planning and monitoring. Your expansion plan and its implementation need to recognise that people have differing reactions to change and that they need to be involved in the change process. You need to talk to people, listen to what they say and to involve them in the decision-taking process. Use the converted sceptics from the pilot trial – they can be powerful advocates for change. You also need to make sure that your implementation or expansion of this gap-closing option will lead to a success that's stable and permanent by:

- providing enough appropriate support and resources
- hand-picking the people involved,
- empowering those people so that they can get results

The next step

You'll feel good when the results start to come in. You've reached your goal – maybe even exceeded it . The people that you've worked with will be proud of the results that they've achieved. You might get other business units asking you how you did it. You're basking in the glow of having accomplished what you set out to achieve. This is the point at which you need to remind yourself that successful performance management isn't a one-shot effort. It's a continuous on-going process. No matter how good the results you measure and monitor, no matter how well your customers like your products or services – there's always room for improvement. If you sit back rest, on your laurels, you'll get overtaken. You'll slip back down the greasy pole to where you started. Getting back up will be twice as difficult. This will happen because:

- new methods, equipment or technologies appear all the time, making your 'new' option out-of-date and obsolete
- your customers will expect more
- your people's skills will change – they'll be able to do more and do it better
- your 'new' option will degrade, gradually lose its cutting edge over time
- there will always be a better way to do it.

What you need to do – even if things are going perfectly – is to challenge the 'status quo'. Start asking your people what they'd do if a key machine broke down or a key person went sick. Ask about the 'gap-closing' options that you didn't trial – are they still low ranking or has new technology or lower or higher costs changed that situation? You need to get dissatisfied. You need to reach out for new goals and targets. One of the ways that you can do that is by using benchmarks.

Benchmarks and benchmarking

What are they?
Benchmarks are measured standards. They represent 'best practice' for a task or activity. A benchmark can come from anywhere. It can be from any industry or any country – even from within your own company. But the benchmarks that you use on your road to successful performance management must be about the same sort of function or task that your business unit carries out. There's no point, as they say, in comparing apples with pears.

Using benchmarks helps you to:

- get to know and understand the sort of activities that go on in your business unit
- understand how the competition's doing it
- find the best ways of carrying out those activities
- use those 'best ways' in your business unit.

How can you use benchmarks?

Doing this isn't only easier than you'd expect, it's also very informative. These benchmarks can be applied to any or all of the operations that go on in your business unit. For example, when Xerox was searching for benchmarks, it identified a wide range of organizations that represented the best performance for the sort of activities that took place in Xerox. These activities included warehouse operations, document processing, bill scanning, service parts provision, information systems and automated assembly. But these organizations weren't Xerox's competitors – they included vehicle and clothing manufacturers, banking and finance houses. Their products or services had nothing to do with Xerox's products. So, when Xerox checked out their warehouse operations, they looked at warehouse operations of LL Bean, an American outdoor clothes manufacturer. When they did this they found that Bean's warehouse operations – which were comparable and outstanding – packed things three times quicker than their warehouse. Xerox used this information to improve their own warehouse operations. Using bench marks as performance targets or goals can be a powerful and important step on your road to successful performance management. It's a continuous rather than an occasional process. When you do it, you compare your business unit's performance in specific activities to the best for those activities. Then you set your performance goals for that activity.

Benchmarks:
- tell you what the standards of excellence are
- provide you with realistic goals and targets to work towards
- help you to understand how you can improve.

Benchmarks – where from?
The benchmarks that you use can come from:

- your competitors
- 'world class' organizations
- the best within your own organization.

Getting competitive and world class benchmarks can require a lot of research and analysis while internal benchmarks usually don't. These 'home grown' benchmarks are also easier to transfer because of:

- the absence of any confidentiality constraints on 'know – how ' transfer
- ease of access to people who are experienced in the process or activity which generates the benchmark.

However, internal benchmarks can suffer from lack of credibility. They will also need to be compared with competitor performance. Getting to know how well your competitor is doing it and finding out what the 'world class' benchmarks are is worthwhile. They'll give you a glimpse of ways of doing things that aren't just new and innovative – they've also been tried and tested.

Benchmarks – how long?
Benchmarking isn't an instant process. It often takes four to six weeks to set a benchmarking project and it can take even longer to build links and trust with benchmarking partners. Experience indicates that a first-time benchmarking project can take between six and nine months to complete – depending on its 'what' and the 'who'. But after that initial period, it's only up-dating that is needed and your benchmarking project will become an on-going activity.

Benchmarking – success or failure?
If you want to make sure that your benchmarking is a success then you'll need to:

- choose the right measure and the right partner
- get senior management support and adequate resources
- start and stay small – don't benchmark too many measures

To get more information about benchmarking and sources of benchmarks take a look at *Understanding Benchmarking in a Week*.

Summary

Today, you've looked at what you can do with the results that you get from your performance measurement and monitoring. You've seen how you can use those results to identify and achieve the goals, targets and benchmarks of your successful performance management. Tomorrow you'll be looking at some of the tools and techniques that help you in your successful performance management. In the meantime here's a summary of Thursday:

- Successful performance management goals, targets and benchmarks are about closing the gap between where you are and where you want to be.
- You need to:
  - identify that gap and find out what its cause is
  - look at options for closing that gap
  - select one, trial or test it and then review the results

- modify or reject the option as required
- implement that action.
- make your gap-closing option a permanent feature of your operation or apply it in other areas or on a larger scale.
- Doing this should be a continuous, on-going process
- Benchmarks
  - tell you what the standards of excellence are
  - provide you with realistic goals and targets to work towards
  - help you to understand how you can improve.

Successful performance management techniques

Today you'll take a look at some techniques to help you on your way to your successful performance management. By the end of the day you should have a better understanding of some techniques that you can use to recognise and understand the problems that you'll meet on that journey. You'll also, just as importantly, have seen tools and techniques that you can use to identify potential solutions to those problems. When you've done that, you'll have looked at the following:

- Techniques or tools?
- Moving averages
- Cumulative sums
- Pareto principle
- Input – output diagrams
- Ishikawa diagrams

WILL COLOURED PAPERCLIPS HELP US TO MEET OUR TARGETS, NIGEL?

Techniques or tools?

Techniques are really tools. They're a means of doing or achieving something. The something that you want to achieve is successful performance management. There's quite a range of tools that you can use to get to that. You've already come across situations where tools will help you to:

- measure and monitor – moving averages, cumulative sum (CUSUM) plots
- analyse – Pareto analysis, Ishikawa and influence diagrams.

Tools and techniques can also help you solve your problems. Problems and performance management seem to go together like ham and eggs or bread and butter. These problems range from the large to the small and from the certain and clear to the uncertain and obscure. Their consequences extend from the significant to the trifling.

Today you'll look at a limited number of tools and techniques. They have been chosen because they are straight-forward and practical, as well as robust enough for everyday use. You don't have to be a rocket scientist to use them. However, as is so with all tools, the skill is in their use – and that will lie with you. Once you've got used to using these, you'll be ready to try using some more sophisticated ones. You can find these by looking in books on problems solving.

Moving averages

The moving average tells you how something you're measuring moves up and down with time. You calculate it this way:

1 Get the values for whatever it is that you're measuring for four time periods, weeks, days, months.
2 Add these together and divide by four. This gives the arithmetic average value for those four periods.
3 When the value for the fifth period is available, add this to the previous total and then subtract the value for the first period.
4 Divide this new total by four. This gives you the average for periods two through to five. This is the moving average.
5 Continue generating these moving averages as in steps 3 and 4 and plot the results you get on a graph. If you want, you can also plot the original values for each time period on the same graph.

The moving average is a useful and simple tool that:

• tells you whether what you are measuring is drifting up or down
• helps you to monitor what's happening
• damps or smoothes out any seasonal variations or violent ups and downs that might mislead you
• requires limited training for its use.

However, because it looks at 'smoothed' averages for a period of time, using the moving average technique may mean that you don't spot a change until sometime after it has happened. If you need to make sure that this doesn't happen then use the next technique – the cumulative sum or CUSUM technique.

Cumulative sums

The cumulative sum or CUSUM technique also tells you if something is moving up and down with time. But – unlike the moving average technique – it will detect early shifts or movements. When you use the CUSUM technique you compare your measured value to a previously established target. You then graph the running cumulative sum of the differences between these. This is how you do that:

1 Establish the target for what you're measuring. This can be a desired value or an historic average value.
2 Take the first measured value and subtract from this target value. The difference will be negative or positive and you use it to begin the cumulative sum of the differences.
3 Start your graph of this cumulative sum.
4 Repeat step 2 for each value you measure. Add the new difference to your cumulative sum and then plot the new value of that cumulative sum on your graph.

This CUSUM graph will show you a change in the measured value:

- when it happens
- in a way which is not damped by 'smoothing'

This happens because the change causes the slope of the CUSUM graph to change. However, care must be taken in the choice of scales for your CUSUM graph as a large difference could push points off the scale.

Pareto principle

The Pareto principle is often called the 80/20 or 70/30 rule. It says that, in any group, there are a minority of things, people or events that cause the majority of the effects or consequences. That is, for example, that 80% of your sales revenue comes from 20% of your products or 70% of your quality problems come from 30% of your operators. In your performance management, these effects or consequences could be about anything – costs, turnover, energy usage, the number of complaints made or staff time usage. In stock control situations, Pareto analysis is often called the ABC technique. This tells you that some of your stock items (A items) have much higher turnovers or sales revenues than other slower moving or lower sales level items (B and C items). These A items require tight control of stock levels, reorder quantities, etc. In short, Pareto analysis gives you leverage in your problem solving. It helps you to identify those activities, items or problem areas in which the minimum of effort will produce the maximum gain.

Pareto analysis

1 Assemble your data. It's relative performance or effect, rather than absolute accuracy, that's important here. So make sure that all of the data you use has

the same level of accuracy and is for the same period of time.

2 Identify and calculate the factor that you're going to use to compare the contribution or effect of the items in your data group. You can do this by multiplying, adding or subtracting data for individual items. For example, the annual sales revenue will be generated by multiplying sales volume by item price while the profit might be generated by subtracting production costs from sales revenue.

3 Generate a table for the comparison factor of each item with the largest value at the top, the rest in descending order below.

4 Calculate and add to this table the total for the comparison factor, the percentages of that total for each item's comparison factor value and the cumulative total of these percentages.

5 Identify those items that lie below the 80% cumulative total level in the above table. You can do this by plotting a graph of the cumulative percentages against the cumulative number or percentage of items.

These are the 20% that cause the 80% of the comparison factor. Having found them you'll now subject them to more detailed analysis or monitoring. The object of that analysis and monitoring will be to identify and eliminate the causes of problems or weaknesses. In the example overleaf you'll see that:

- items f and d account for 76.59% of this total
- items f, d and g account for 89.54% of this total.

As their contribution to sales revenue is some seven to nine times greater than that of the remaining items, either of these groups could be the focus of further analysis and monitoring.

Pareto analysis example

Steps 1 and 2	Item	Unit price (£)	Annual sales (000s)	Annual revenue (£)
	a	30	2.67	80,100
	b	12	4.18	50,160
	c	450	0.2	90,000
	d	75	20	1,500,000
	e	1500	0.5	750,000
	f	800	7.0	5,600,000
	g	200	6.0	1,200,000

Steps 3 and 4	Item	Annual revenue (£)	% of annual revenue	Cumulative % of annual revenue
	f	5,600,000	60.41	60.41
	d	1,500,000	16.18	76.59
	g	1,200,000	12.94	89.54
	e	750,000	8.09	97.63
	c	90,000	0.97	98.60
	a	80,100	0 .86	99.46
	b	50,160	0.54	100.00
	Total:	9,270,260		

Cumulative % of annual revenue

Cumulative % of items

Input-output diagrams

This sort of diagram will help you to identify the resources that flow in and out of a business unit or process. Creating one focuses your attention on what these are and what their importance or size is. The first key step in creating an input-output diagram is to make sure that you have identified all the inputs and all the outputs for the process. If you fail to do this, not only will you have an incomplete diagram, you'll also have one that's of little use to you. This need to be comprehensive is illustrated in the figure below that shows the input-output diagram for the process of making a cup of tea. This diagram shows that you can:

- improve efficiency by reducing excess milk, infusion and hot water
- enhance effectiveness by making sure the tea is made when and it's required
- improve adaptability by ensuring that tea is to the 'required' strength every time and for every customer.

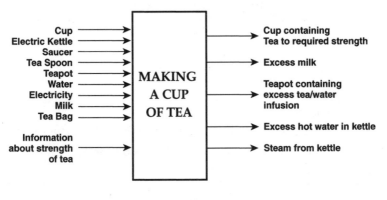

Ishikawa diagrams

Basics
The Ishikawa diagram is often also called the 'fishbone' or 'cause and effect' diagram. It provides you with a powerful and comprehensive way of identifying possible causes of your problems. The diagram (see below) starts with you drawing a box on the right hand side of a sheet of paper. In this box you write the problem to be solved. You then draw an arrow across the sheet, pointing towards the box, and further arrows pointing towards and joining the main arrow. Each of these side arrows represents a family or group of causes which could have led to the problem. These side arrows are usually labelled with 5Ms: Machinery, Manpower, Methods, Material and Maintenance. If you want, you can extend these to the 6Ms , by the addition of Mother Nature, or shrink them to the 4Ms by taking out Maintenance.

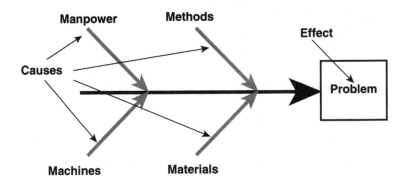

How and when
You can generate a cause and effect or Ishikawa diagram on your own or do it in a group. However you do it, the basic steps are still the same:

1 Clearly define the problem.
2 Identify all possible causes by brainstorming. Generate lists of causes, rather than solutions.
3 Group the causes generated under the 4, 5 or 6M headings.
4 Visually connect all causes back to the problem using the fishbone diagram. You may need to condense the cause descriptions at this stage.
5 Use the diagram to continue the identification of possible causes until all of these, even the improbable ones, have been written down.
6 Review the diagram and decide which of the causes are to be investigated first.

This diagram, if used well, will give you a comprehensive list of all possible causes. The figure below shows how the technique could be applied – using the 4M headings – to the problem of a cup of tea that's too strong.

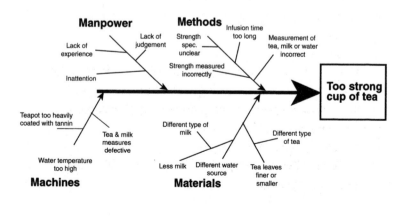

You can use other tools – such as the 'Five Whys' – to help you to create your Ishikawa diagram. This starts by asking why the problem has occurred and getting an answer that might be, for example, 'because component A failed.' You then ask 'why did component A fail?' and get answer 'because—'. By the time you have asked 'why?' five times you will usually find you have arrived at the root cause of the problem.

Summary

Today you've looked at some of the techniques and tools that will help you to your successful performance management. Tomorrow you'll start by looking at how important it is to make sure that the goals and targets of your performance management are compatible with the long-term goals or strategy of your organization. You'll also review where you've got to in this week. Here's a summary of Friday:

- Techniques are tools.
- These tools will help you to –
  - measure and monitor
  - analyse
  - solve problems.
- Moving averages and CUSUMs will help monitor the way what you're measuring moves up and down.
- Input-output diagrams help decide what to adjust to upgrade your business unit's efficiency, effectiveness or adaptability.
- Ishikawa diagrams help identify the possible cause of your problems.

The long view and review

Over the last six days you've looked at the ways and means of achieving your own version of successful performance management. On this, the last day of your week, you'll see that performance management isn't just about the short-term, day-by-day aspects of your workplace. For your performance management must support the long view of where your organization is going. This – as you'll soon see – is its strategy. When you've done that you'll have looked at:

- What is strategy?
- Decisions, decisions and decisions
- Strategy and performance management
- From broad to fine
- Single or double?
- Russian dolls

Finally, you'll remind yourself about the week's key points of successful performance management.

What is strategy?

All organizations, whatever their origins, age or history, have objectives. These can be about things like becoming the dominant car maker in Europe or reducing world poverty. What these organizations want, above all, is to:

- achieve these objectives, and
- survive the cut and thrust of the market place.

In order to do that, they have to take decisions and make plans about the 'what', 'why' and 'when' of their future actions. The goals, targets, schemes and plans that result from these decisions are called their strategies.

Decisions, decisions and decisions

But these aren't the only decisions that get taken in organizations. In your workplace you decide things like what's to be done, when it's to be done and who will do it – all on a day-by-day or hour-by-hour basis. Hand-books about management call these the administrative and operating decisions. They are, as you know, the sort of decisions that are:

- taken regularly, frequently and routinely
- concerned with a part, rather than the whole, of the organization
- about the short or medium-term time-scale
- concerned with the use of limited resources
- taken by middle managers or below.

The strategic decisions of your organization are different. These reflect the ambitions and aspirations of those who lead that organization. They are concerned with a vision of where that organization might be be in the future. They are about the what, why and when of that vision.

These strategic decisions are about the 'game-plan' of your organisation. They are:

- taken periodically
- about the whole organization and its long-term objectives
- concerned with the way the organization responds to the market place and other external influences
- taken by very senior managers

Strategy and performance management

So what's the connection between these infrequent, high level 'game-plan' or strategic decisions and the nitty–gritty of your day-by-day performance management? How do they influence each other? The answer, if you think about it, is quite obvious. It also comes in two parts.

The first part of this answer lies in the fact that your business unit's perfomance management measurements are a part of the starting point of your organization's strategy. They define where that organization has been and where it currently is. They provide the foundations of the launch pad for the strategies of your organization's future. But, secondly and just as importantly, it's your successful performance management that is the key to shifting your organizations

strategy from the 'hoped–for' to the 'achieved'. Once that
strategy has been chosen, once it has been decided, it's your
successful performance management that enables it to
become real.

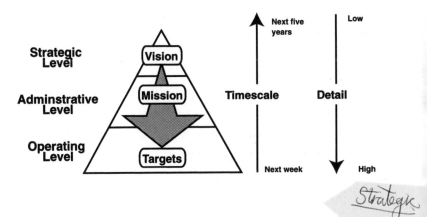

From broad to fine

But how does that happen? How do you get from the fine
detail of the day-to-day, hour-to-hour decisions that you take
in your business unit to the broad span, long-term strategy
of, say, becoming the dominant car manufacturer in Europe.
Again, there are two parts of the answer to this question and
you'll now look at each of them in turn.

Single or double?
You saw on Wednesday that when you measure the
performance of your business unit you compare it to a goal,
target or standard. If the measured performance is below that
standard you take action to raise it. If it's above it, you'll
probably need to find out why – so that you can keep it up
there. This single loop of actions looks something like the one

in the diagram on the left below.

But what if the target needs to change – because a different strategy is needed for the business as a whole? This is where

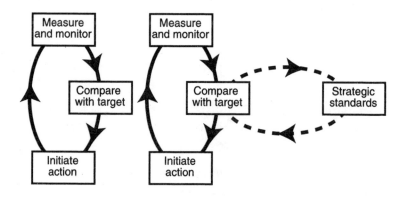

the second loop comes in – as you can see in the diagram on the right above. This double loop enables you and your organization to make sure that the goals of your business unit are in tune with and compatible with the targets of the organization as a whole.

Russian dolls

You're all familiar with those Russian dolls. They're the ones that you twist in the middle and they open to reveal another doll inside. When you twist that doll it also opens. On and on it goes, with dolls inside dolls inside dolls inside dolls inside dolls until you get to the tiny doll at the centre – the one that won't twist open. The goals and targets that cascade down from the high level strategic targets of your organization to your business unit are rather like these dolls. They nest inside each other. When you open one up it reveals another related

target inside. All of these have to be integrated and
compatible with:

- the organization's overarching strategic goals and
  targets,
- each other.

Nested targets

Here's a simple example of a set of 'nested' targets:

Level	Target
Organization	To be the dominant car manufacturer in Europe.
Division	To design and manufacture sports cars that sell in volume and contribute 10% of the organization's turnover and 20% of its profit
Works	To profitably manufacture AZ Sports car.
Department	To assemble AZ Sports car efficiently and effectively.
Shop	To efficiently coat and paint bodies for AZ Sports car as demanded by production schedules.

Each of these levels has a different goal. But, in order to
achieve that goal, all of the goals in the levels below must
also be achieved – and that can only be achieved by
successful performance management.

Looking back over the week

Sunday

On Sunday you first came across the key elements of successful performance management. You found that they are:

- people
- quality
- measuring and monitoring
- goals, targets and benchmarks
- techniques.

You also met the ten commandments of successful performance management:

1   Successful performance management is no longer an optional extra.

2   Successful performance management means accepting and embracing change – rather than holding it at arm's length.

3   Successful performance management is a continuous and on-going process rather than a one-off project.

4   Performance management is a 'people centred' activity.

5   Successful performance management is done *with* people, not *to* them.

6   Successful performance management is driven by the gap between where you are now and where you want to be.

7   Successful performance management measures are credible and understandable.

8   Successful performance management measures
    are about efficiency, effectiveness and adaptability.
9   Successful performance management uses
    techniques that are relevant and effective – and
    uses them well.
10 The ultimate judges of your performance
    management are your customers – and they
    deserve to be delighted.

Monday

On Monday you looked in detail at the people aspects of
successful performance management. What you saw was that:

- People are core to successful performance
  management
- Successful performance management is done *with*
  people – rather than *to* them
- Do this, and do it well, and you'll need to:
  - manage change effectively
  - tap into people's creativity and energy
  - solve problems with solutions that benefit
    everybody.
- Teams and projects will help you to do that.
- Teams make things happen – quicker and better –
  and find ways of moving your performance
  management up a gear.
- The project is one of the tools that can help you
  achieve success in your performance management.
- To achieve success in your performance
  management you and your people will need more
  and different skills.

- Training can give you these skills – provided it's based on an accurate and honest assessment of what you need.

Tuesday

On Tuesday you looked at quality and the role that it plays in successful performance management. What you saw was that:

- Quality is fitness for purpose or use.
- Anything can possess quality providing its purpose is clearly defined and its performance meets that definition.
- The steps to quality involve identifying customer need, deciding which part of that need you're going to answer, detailing the answer to that need and designing and creating the answer
- Internal and external customers are both important.
- Total quality management (TQM) is a way of managing organizations
- QA systems are about delighting your customer – consistently.
- Most common fallacies about quality don't stand up to examination.
- Getting it right means being there for the long haul and involving everyone as well as embracing change, having a vision of where you're going and using measurables to monitor your progress.
- Most quality gurus tell us that it's the management of quality that's important – rather than it's control.

Wednesday

Wednesday was the day on which you looked at the way that measurement and monitoring can contribute to the success of your performance management. You saw that:

- Measures give you feedback on how you're performing
- Measures need to be –
  - easily understood
  - easily generated
  - inexpensive to measure
  - near to the 'action'
  - motivating
  - directly related to customer satisfaction.
- Measures also need to be accessible and credible.
- Measurement systems can focus on –
  - efficiency – or resource utilisation
  - effectiveness – whether you give your customer the 'right' service at the 'right' place and time
  - adaptability – really answering the needs of your customers.
- The 'when', 'where' and 'who' of your measurement system are key to its effectiveness.
- You need to monitor your measures, analyse their information and use it to keep your business unit on course.
- Planning the how and when of your measurement and monitoring is vital.
- Starting small and growing leads to success.

Thursday

By the time Thursday came around, you were ready to look at what you can do with the results of your performance measurement and monitoring. You saw that you can use them to identify and achieve the goals, targets and benchmarks of your successful performance management. You saw that:

- Successful performance management goals, targets and benchmarks are about helping you to close the gap between where you are and where you want to be
- You need to –
  - identify that gap
  - find out what its cause is
  - look at options for closing that gap
  - select one and trial or test it
  - review trial's results
  - modify or reject the option as required
  - implement that action
  - make your gap-closing option a permanent feature of your operation or apply it in other areas or on a larger scale.
- Doing this should be a continuous on-going process.
- Benchmarks can –
  - tell you what the standards of excellence are
  - provide you with realistic goals and targets to work towards
  - help you to understand how you can improve.

Friday

On Friday you looked at some of the techniques of successful performance management . You saw:

- Techniques are tools.
- These tools will help you to –

- measure and monitor
- analyse
- solve problems.
- Moving averages and CUSUMs will help monitor the way what you're measuring moves up and down.
- Input-output diagrams help decide what to adjust to upgrade your business unit's efficiency, effectiveness or adaptability.
- Ishikawa diagrams help identify the possible cause of your problems.

Saturday

In the early part of Saturday, you looked at strategy and found that:

- Strategy is about an organization's overarching goals, targets and ambitions
- Strategic decisions are –
  - taken periodically
  - about the whole organization and its long-term objectives
  - concerned with the way the organization responds to the market place and other external influences taken by very senior managers.
- The goals and targets of your performance management must be compatible with the organization's strategy if you are going to be successful.

Conclusion

Gaining success in your performance management isn't easy. The road to it demands hard work, thought, dedication and commitment. Doing all this will ask far more of you than standing still or maintaining the status quo. But it is worthwhile. For successful performance management will boost your bottom line, delight your customers, motivate and 'turn-on' the people you work with and – just as importantly – help your career. But that's not all that it will do. For, as you saw earlier in this book, success in your performance management will bring other, just-as-important, benefits. For it will be:

- an act of empowerment for you and those you work with.

- an opportunity for you to grow, develop and change.

- an opportunity for you organisation to be successful.

And that can't be bad!

Here are some other books that may also help you on your road to successful performance management:

- Leadership in a Week
- Operations Management in a Week   **Chartered Management Institute in a Week series**
- Negotiating in a Week
- Strategy in a Week
- Project Management in a Week
- Teach Yourself Project Management
- Teach Yourself Negotiating.   **Teach Yourself series**
- Teach Yourself Teams and Teamworking